XL MACHINES!

# DUMP TRUCKS

MARIE MORRISON

New York

Published in 2020 by The Rosen Publishing Group, Inc.
29 East 21st Street, New York, NY 10010



First Edition

Editor: Greg Roza
Book Design: Michael Flynn

Photo Credits: Cover, p. 1 kaband/Shutterstock.com; series background (dirt) exopixel/Shutterstock.com; p. 5 Dmytro Budnik/Shutterstock.com; p. 7 5m3photos/Shutterstock.com; p. 9 FrimuFilms/Shuttersock.com; p. 11 Sunshine Seeds/Shutterstock.com; p. 13 TFoxFoto/Shutterstock.com; p. 15 Zacarias Pereira da Mata/Shutterstock.com; p. 17 LeitWolf/Shutterstock.com; p. 19 XRISTOFOROV/Shutterstock.com; p. 21 C Levers/Shutterstock.com; p. 22 Eric Milos/Shutterstock.com.

Cataloging-in-Publication Data

Names: Morrison, Marie.
Title: Dump trucks / Marie Morrison.
Description: New York : PowerKids Press, 2020. | Series: XL machines! | Includes glossary and index.
Identifiers: ISBN 9781725311466 (pbk.) | ISBN 9781725311480 (library bound) | ISBN 9781725311473 (6pack)
Subjects: LCSH: Dump trucks--Juvenile literature.
Classification: LCC TL230.15 M677 2020 | DDC 629.224-dc23

Manufactured in the United States of America

CPSIA Compliance Information: Batch #CSPK19. For Further Information contact Rosen Publishing, New York, New York at 1-800-237-9932.

# CONTENTS

## Useful Machines

What would we do without dump trucks? These extra-large machines move a lot of dirt and other matter from place to place. After a dump truck moves something, its body can tip to dump its load out.

193

## Why So Big?

Dump trucks are so big because they need to move big loads. Many of the things they carry, such as rocks, are very heavy. Dump trucks need large **engines**. They often have more than four wheels. They might have up to 12!

## Parts of a Dump Truck

The area where a dump truck carries things is called the bed. A **hinge** is at the back of the truck. Pistons, which are parts that slide up and down, lift the bed to dump the truck's load.

pistons

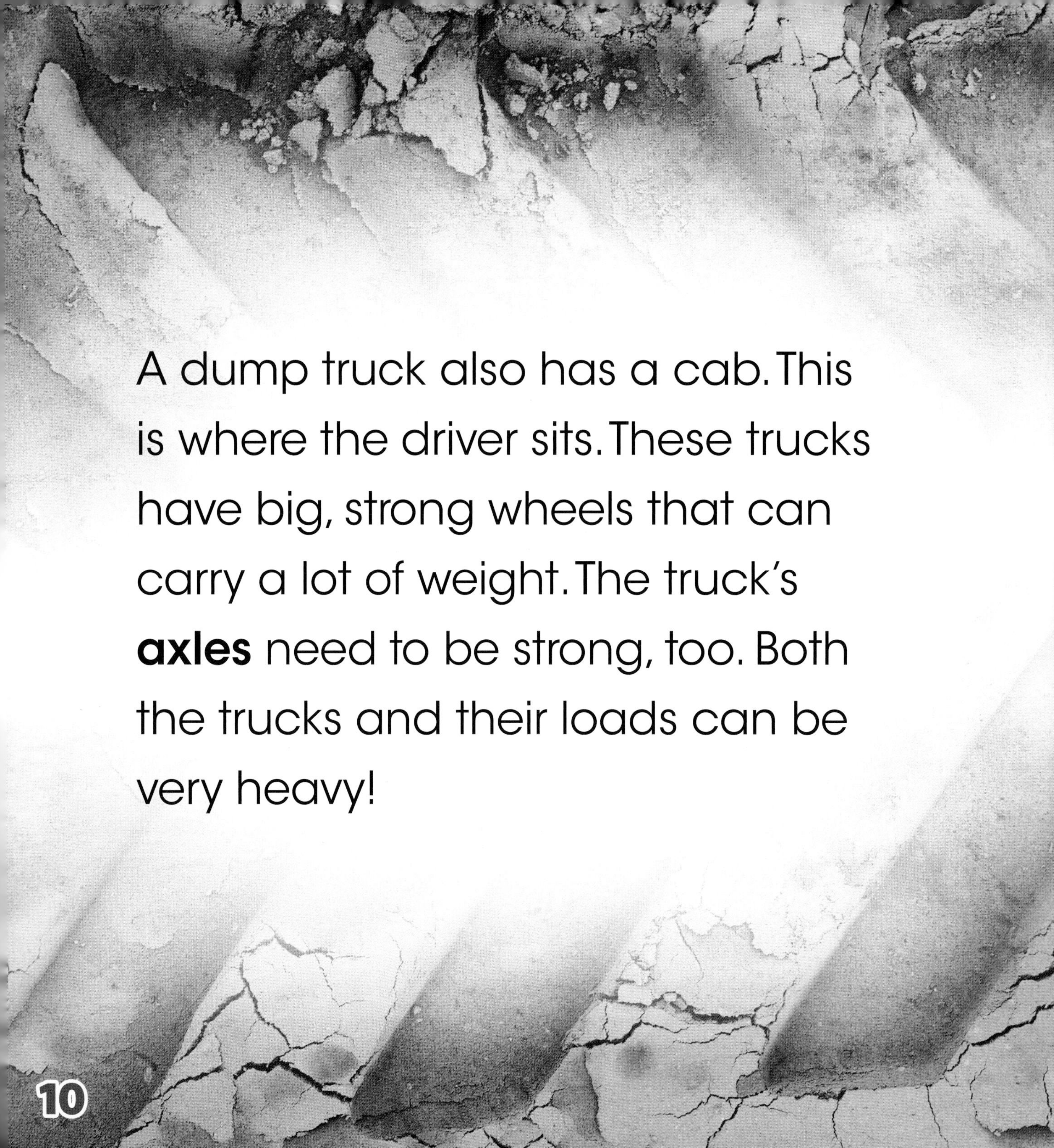

A dump truck also has a cab. This is where the driver sits. These trucks have big, strong wheels that can carry a lot of weight. The truck's **axles** need to be strong, too. Both the trucks and their loads can be very heavy!

cab

## Dumping Differences

Not all dump trucks are the same. They come in different sizes. They also work in different ways. Some dump their load to the side instead of to the back. Some have extra **cargo** areas so they can carry more.

## What and Where

Where do you think you can find dump trucks? You can see them around **construction** sites. They move building **materials** to and from these places where people are building things. You can see some very big dump trucks at mining sites.

## The Biggest Truck

All dump trucks are big, but some are huge! A dump truck called the BelAZ 75710 works at a mine in Siberia. It's 67.5 feet (20.6 m) long—that's about as long as two school buses parked end to end!

BELAZ 75710
75710
450
ТОНН

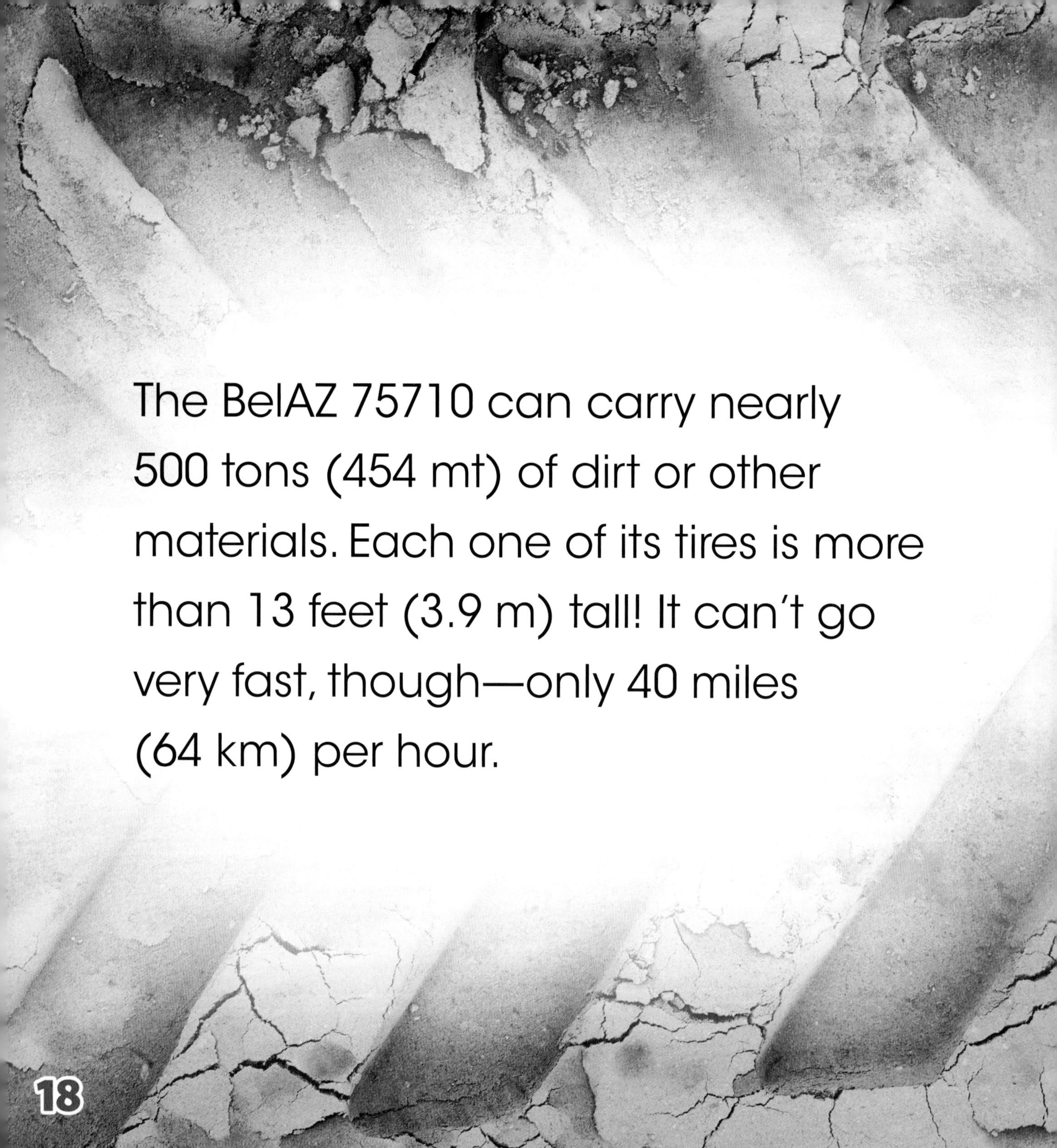

The BelAZ 75710 can carry nearly 500 tons (454 mt) of dirt or other materials. Each one of its tires is more than 13 feet (3.9 m) tall! It can't go very fast, though—only 40 miles (64 km) per hour.

BELAZ 75710
75710
BELAZ
450
TOHH
BELAZ

## Extra-Large Toys

Real dump trucks are huge, but you might see small ones, too—in your room or your yard! A company called Tonka is famous for making toy dump trucks. In the beginning, these were very heavy. Even the toys weighed about 11 pounds (5 kg) each!

## Make It Possible

It's no surprise that many people find dump trucks interesting. Without them, it'd be a lot harder to build and move things! These extra-large machines carry huge loads and make it possible for us to make tall buildings, smooth roads, and more.

# GLOSSARY

**axle:** The bar on which a wheel turns.

**cargo:** Goods carried by a plane, train, or truck.

**construction:** Having to do with the act of building something.

**engine:** A machine that turns fuel, such as gasoline, into movement.

**hinge:** A piece, often metal, that attaches something to something else and allows it to move.

**material:** Something from which something else can be made.

# INDEX



# WEBSITES

Due to the changing nature of Internet links, PowerKids Press has developed an online list of websites related to the subject of this book. This site is updated regularly. Please use this link to access the list: www.powerkidslinks.com/xlm/dumptrucks